Leaving Grief at Heaven's Gate

Leaving Grief at Heaven's Gate

Sorrow No More: God's Grace Reigns Over Grief

Theresa Ellison

XULON PRESS

Xulon Press
2301 Lucien Way #415
Maitland, FL 32751
407.339.4217
www.xulonpress.com

Printed in the United States of America.

ISBN-13: 978-1-6322-1339-6
Ebook: 978-1-6322-1340-2

Author's website:
www.blessmyblog.com

This book is faithfully dedicated to:

My only Lord Jesus Christ for His Glory and Praise.

My husband and best friend, Steve whose enduring precious love for me has sent me to higher aspirations that would never be possible without him.

My son Adam who inspires me with his fearless risks and gifted success.

My son Alex who encompasses ingenious ideas and makes courageous choices.

My stepson Josh who carries out his dreams.

My cousin Susan and friend Laureen who encourage me.

My German Shepherd Sheba who faithfully displays unconditional love and friendship.

Table of Contents

Leaving Grief at Heaven's Gate
An Introduction to Healing Grace

Have you been told to welcome your grief and experience all the stages and emotions included within your journey? If you have encountered a professional, a book, or a blog that encourages healing in this manner, please read on.

As a professional counselor and chaplain, I have witnessed people approach healing from a symptom management and educational perspective. Talk therapy, emotional regulation, thought replacement, exercise, journaling, medications, and grief groups hold a place while offering limited relief. However, it is a common error in practice for professionals to encourage the bereaved to embrace their grief. What benefit is there to roll out the welcome mat for something that only steals a sound mind and serves negative symptoms?

I find it a double standard to recommend that healing grief is achieved through an invitation of acceptance. Recognition of grief is there, even if it is buried deep within the heart. Denial is protection from the pain; it doesn't defer the healing unless the right physician is allowed in. The facets or stages of grief being greeted into the hurting life hold no power. Think about it—do doctors tell a cancer patient to accept the cancer and embrace the disease? Hardly so. They work out a treatment plan to quickly rid you of such poison. If you, like many, feel grief has taken up residence within your soul without your permission, it is no coincidence you are reading this book. Let us waste no time and begin to dig into the deeper side of grief and discover your source of healing.

The Force of Grief

Grief is forceful. It has power to rob peace and place one into a hopeless abyss. Feeling stuck with unwanted symptoms sends a person into a frantic search. Finding the right source can be as exhausting as the grief itself. Scoping out the internet or the local paper for experts in grief counseling also leads one to wonder who can be trusted. Investing time in choosing the right person and providing your history and circumstances surrounding the loss only to find the counselor is not a match is risky. If you do find a trustworthy counselor, the sessions may help normalize your grief, but do not fully heal your heart's pain. Education alone makes one a smarter grieving person. Don't get me wrong; there is much benefit within the practice of professional help as well as the general knowledge of what grief entails (remember, I am a professional counselor). Allow me to explain.

If you purchased a clock from someone who personally built it and it broke, wouldn't you want to return the item to the maker for repair? Rather than run to the common resources within this world to fix your broken heart, leave it in the hands of the designer. Maybe you are unaware that your creator has already rectified your grief problem. First we must go back to where grief was born.

Where Grief was Born

We will begin at the birthplace of grief. Grief was born out of a garden called Eden. Adam and Eve walked through paradise without a sorrowful stone to stumble upon. That is, until an evil fallen angel, Satan, came to visit. He baited Eve with the lie that eating the fruit from the Tree of Knowledge was not a problem. Eve was deceived and offered Adam a taste. The juicy fruit they ingested was the first connection to the spirit of sorrow. Aligning themselves with the devil's world resulted in rebellion against God, turning their paradise into a funeral parlor. Separation from the very source of peace, love, and joy, Adam and Eve experienced great loss. Death was now the new course they chose, which offered no insurance plan of eternal life with the Father.

Talk about depression introduced in a day. Adam and Eve were stuck in Satan's crafty plan to rule over the Father's creation. If this was my plight I would wrap up in a blanket and hide forever. Sounds like grief to me. However, the love and compassion that a perfect Father has upon His children doesn't conclude the chapter of paradise. God sent His son Jesus to pay the legal penalty to redeem them back from Satan's domain. From a baby in the manger to a man on the cross, more work was accomplished than the human eye could ever behold. It is here, my grieving friend, that your answer lies.

Peer with me and ponder the Scriptures which promise hope to your heart. Jesus bled for your brokenness. He destroyed the dark principalities and powers that bind you with sorrow. Grappling with grief is no longer your business. The work has been finished by the Son of Man through the power of the Holy Spirit. So why do people think they need to work through grief and all the stages it presents when Jesus already accomplished it?

I am now speaking the language of grace. Grace gives you everything you need to be returned to the Father's perfect love. Grace gives you the keys to enter into the kingdom of God and partake in all His goodness. Grace is a gift; all you need to do is receive. Jesus is the grace that grants you permission to leave your grief at the gates of Heaven. You have no power to heal it, deal with it, work it in or out of your life. Jesus has already brought peace to this very sorrow you suffer. I invite you to experience the fullness of His grace.

Lack of Knowledge

The snare of the devil is to keep you out of the loop. If you are unaware of your inheritance, how can you receive it? Keeping a will hidden won't produce the power of receiving what it reads. The deep truths of the cross have been sheltered from well-meaning believers. It is time to shine the light and set the bereaved free.

How many of us have been taught that Jesus took away our sins to grant us forgiveness? We seem to receive that aspect of the work on the cross, but many go shy of what else they can be saved from. Let the Word of God reveal to your spirit that His salvation includes sorrow. See Isaiah 53 and 63. Look at the great exchange here. Peace for sorrow? It doesn't take a rocket scientist to discover this is a great deal. I am amazed at how many people would rather stay stuck with sorrow rather than receive God's relief. That is another lie that the devil cleverly plants into vulnerable minds.

Emotion is a powerful connector. If you have a great first date and walk away with a pocketful of adrenaline, I am sure you will meet again. But what about people who seem to like misery? We assume only positive emotions create a bond. Not so. A person sitting at the bedside of his or her loved one can experience deep regret, guilt, sadness, anger, and fear. When the loved one dies, this is the last emotion they remember that has connection with the deceased. If a person associates grievous emotions with the relationship, these poisonous feelings have a circuit for connection. Ignorance keeps the devastating feelings fueled.

This is why grieving people feel guilty if comfort flickers a sign of hope. They fear they will lose closeness with or even dishonor their loved ones by letting their grief feelings resolve. Grief has the ability to overpower one's perspective. Sound judgment is clouded. It takes sorting through the deception with God's truth to weed out the lies holding people captive. Jesus has destroyed the power of grief. We who receive His grace also receive His grace over grief.

Conclusion

Our sophisticated system of scholars have missed our Savior in their studies. I am here to bring Jesus back to the throne of theological and psychological debates, and conclude He is the source for healing your grief. Sorrow is a spiritual matter manifesting unrest over God's intended grace.

Whom will you trust? Psychology, theology, theory, or the Bible? As Christ Jesus rose from the dead, He did not take grief with Him into heaven. The work is finished. Leave your grief outside the gate and receive God's grace today.

Grief is a Thief

Hiding under the heavy blankets, a woman wounded with grief wondered why she even woke up. Peeking into the dimly lit room, no glimpse of hope rose to greet her. She felt her life was like a scattered puzzle without a picture on its box. Who would pick up the pieces of her broken heart? Tolerating this confusion had to end. The woman was determined to get out of this depressing darkness. Newly found fury within drove her to get up and face the day.

Grabbing a cup of coffee, she stumbled into her study. The heart broken woman paged through the grief books once again. Reviewing the symptoms of grief made her feel even more discouraged. Yes, she definitely had them all. The authors confirmed she was on the journey of grief, but they somehow forgot to point the way out. The woman spent so much time and energy on grief education only to ask the question; what was she really redeeming? Something was missing, and the woman suddenly felt robbed. Desperate to discover the truth, a stirring within, turned her probing into into prayer. "Oh God, give me understanding. What am I doing wrong? Working on my grief just isn't working." The woman pleaded and pleaded, hoping for an answer.

After a few minutes of prayer, the weary woman glanced over her grief materials. Feeling betrayed and hopeless, she began tossing them one by one onto the floor. Wondering what else she could read, she sorted through the shelves lined with knowledge. The woman stumbled upon her worn-out Bible. Feeling like she had been ignoring an old friend, she began flipping open its pages. Inspiration surged within as a familiar verse caught her eye:

> *The thief cometh not, but for to steal, and to kill, and to destroy: I am come that they might have life, and that they might have it more abundantly. (John 10:10)*

As she mulled over its meaning, a warm glow filled her heart. The grief books were not completely wrong: she was responding as anyone would expect. However, the symptoms of grief were an exact match of the verse she had just read. Grief is actually a thief. Her mind became enlightened. Nowhere in the Bible did God say that the only way out of grief is to grieve. She did not have to allow these negative, destructive emotions to rule her heart and mind. Guilt, depression, anxiety, fatigue, confusion, and hopelessness are not God's will; they are harmful. It dawned on her that rolling out the welcome mat for grief was the problem. Hope and determination drove her to find out how to kick this thief out.

The woman was very familiar with criminals, for she used to counsel them for a living. Contemplating how they operate, she immediately thought about darkness. Crimes are generally committed in the night so nobody can see them. Thieves sneak around and make their way into premises through windows or back doors. The woman recognized grief's entry point was through a lie. She permitted grief in and allowed it to take up residence in her heart. God's Word was shedding light on this evil culprit's ways.

As she was about to search the Scriptures, a disturbing voice interrupted her. She kept hearing it say that she would never feel better. The woman knew it was a lie embedded in grief, trying to steal her peace. Grief kept pounding messages into her mind, telling her she couldn't get rid of its symptoms and to give up trying. She heard in her mind accusations that she was crazy and needed a psychiatrist to medicate her. Grief threw in the old cliché that time would heal her and it was her cross to bear. It was obvious grief worked hard on distracting her from reading what God had to say on the subject. Grief was determined to destroy her.

Praying for a sound mind, the woman again opened God's Word. The eyes of her heart began to open. Light was being shed on the exit plan for this thief.

> *...that God was light, and in him is no darkness at all. (I John 1:5)*

Joy began to permeate her being. This thief of grief could not remain working in dark places where God was welcomed. Truth sank deeper and deeper, pushing the lies out of her mind. Grief was not a friend of God, but an enemy. Jesus destroyed the destroyer on the cross. Disarming all the wicked principalities, Jesus armed her with His delivering power.

> *And having spoiled principalities and powers, he made a shew of them openly, triumphing over them in it. (Colossians 2:15)*

How sneaky this grief was, creeping into her thinking through well-respected authors. Although she believed what God said was true, she listened to counsel that was not in Christ. This was the backdoor the thief used to get into her heart. She was misled with the instruction that she had to welcome grief to find healing. Well, grief had no intention of leaving, nor has it the power to heal. Its purpose is to kill, to rob and to destroy.

> *My people are destroyed for lack of knowledge... (Hosea 4:6)*

Grief left that day and tried hard to get back in, but the woman was wiser now. Her time was spent studying God's Word. Grief could not hold her captive any longer.

> *And ye shall know the truth, and the truth shall make you free. (John 8:32)*

> *To open the blind eyes, to bring out the prisoners from the prison, and them that sit in darkness out of the prison house. (Isaiah 42:7)*

> *For God, who commanded the light to shine out of darkness, hath shined in our hearts, to give the light of the knowledge of the glory of God in the face of Jesus Christ. (II Corinthians 4:6–11)*

Rejection

Let us therefore follow after the things which make for peace, and things wherewith one may edify another. (Romans 14:19)

Stories upon stories are shared involving people who shred the peace when a family member dies. Too often the ugliness of a heart is unleashed when the tender time of grieving needs peace. Underlying resentments seem to arise only to destroy what little unity may remain. The empty space that death creates is no place for grudges to fill in its gaps. But what does one do when the olive branch is rejected and relationships dry up in the midst of such dissention?

When your peace offering is passed over in favor of discord, there comes a time when retreat is wise. What about keeping the peace, you may ask? Isn't that what we are supposed to do? Peacemakers cannot become peacekeepers if the recipient doesn't provide permission for peace in the first place. You cannot possess something that is out of reach. Rejection must be respected, for it is honoring a person's will.

Jesus was accustomed to people's rejection, and He also knew not all peace would be possible. He reached out a hand of love only to have it nailed to the cross.

> *...he was despised, and we esteemed him not. (Isaiah 53: 3)*

Jesus never imposed condemnation on their choice. Rather, He moved on to those who would receive Him. You too need to move toward the ones who love you and leave the haters of your soul in God's hands. While you provide the space, do so without resentment. Speak no evil and love them from afar.

> ***If it be possible,*** *as much as lieth in you, live peaceably with all men. (Romans 12:18)*
>
> *(Emphasis mine)*

As you navigate through grief, immediately give Jesus your hurt to avoid becoming hardened and hateful yourself. A root of bitterness can blur your view of the beauty of forgiveness. No need to focus on the rejection when Jesus battled for your acceptance. Receive God's peace as He triumphs over the wicked powers harming you. Jesus will give you the grace to endure the thorns that prick and prod in and throughout your life. He also imparts upon you the ability to forgive those who offend. Remember, it is only through the power of His presence all of this is made possible.

> *And lest I should be exalted above measure through the abundance of the revelations, there was given to me a thorn in the flesh, the messenger of Satan to buffet me, lest I should be exalted above measure. For this thing I besought the Lord thrice, that it might depart from me. And he said unto me, My grace is sufficient for thee: for my strength is made perfect in weakness. (II Corinthians 12:7–9)*

Irritations

Irritability is a form of anger. Something is violating the boundaries of peace when it begins to surface. People may pass this off as irrelevant since they haven't committed some violent crime. Even though it is more subtle than an outburst of fury, most people don't like its intrusion.

This nagging imposition is a common contender when experiencing a loss. Pushing against inner peace, sadness creates a tension that inevitably trickles into sight. If left ignored, a tiny instigation can set off the spark to a nasty reaction. Nobody enjoys being irritable, and, needless to say, nor do others around them.

Before the fire is lit, find out what is troubling your soul. Grief reactions are multi-faceted, but the root is attached to sadness. When someone dies, there can be melancholy associated with a longing that the deceased was more attentive to you, or feeling disappointed you weren't happier together. Sadness doesn't always mean you had a wonderful relationship. It can be attached to a different type of loss, such as loss of livelihood or wishing the deceased had chosen a different course in life. Therefore, when death invades your peace, search within to what this loss means to you personally.

Identifying the culprit is important, but there is another vital step to take: walk to the Savior who will address the unrest. Recognizing the issue is not enough, for what good is the knowledge if peace has been shattered? Only Jesus can restore wholeness. Allow Him to grant the serenity you require. His limitless supply is waiting to be received.

Peace I leave with you, my peace I give unto you: not as the world giveth, give I unto you. Let not your heart be troubled, neither let it be afraid. (John 14:27)

When you begin to feel annoyed, ask for assistance. The cross of Christ has already purchased your provision. Jesus will gladly serve to replace your irritability with His tranquility.

> *Now the Lord of peace himself give you peace always by all means. (II Thessalonians 3:16)*

> *Peace be unto you. (John 20:19)*

Symptoms

Every day at work, I have to report if I have symptoms of COVID-19 while my temperature is taken. This is a standard precaution to ensure I can attend work. The daily routine raises awareness of my personal health each morning. When you are grieving, it is even more important to monitor your physical health.

During grief, emotional symptoms take priority over the physical body. It is perfectly normal to listen to what screams the loudest. While emotions demand attention in the frontlines of sorrow, it is equally important to give heed to one's body. Grief is very impactful upon your physical health.

If you take into consideration that grief is a major stressor, it is easier to grasp the effect it has upon your entire being. Stress attacks the vulnerable. If you have an old injury, stress sends flares of pain into that spot. Therefore, listen to what your body is saying. It is not selfish to establish self-care. Mourning souls may not feel like attending to their health. Feelings should be reevaluated while grieving. Allow the Scriptures to take precedence and ask for a sound mind (2 Tim. 1:7). As you listen for the Lord's direction, you will develop discernment. Not all feelings are surrendered to the Holy Spirit.

In summary, cooperate with God's Word and guidance. Your body is the temple of the Lord and deserves attention. Follow His lead in developing realistic exercise, diet, sleep, and recreation regimes. Godly habits for health should not be ignored, but included while Jesus heals you from sorrow.

> *Or do you not know that your body is the temple of the Holy Spirit who is in you, whom you have from God, and you are not your own? (I Corinthians 6:19)*

Seeds for a Season

He that soweth the good seed is the Son of man. (Matthew 13:37)

The old man's wrinkles spread an unspoken story across his forlorn face. Gazing upon the fields, the farm calls him back to his younger days. Hard work wears well upon his soul while his body defies its well-known purpose.

Shuffling with a walker hardly resembles the robust stamina he was once acquainted with. The room echoes as boxes are loaded onto the truck. Pain silently pierces within his heart as he realizes the time has come. A soft voice interrupts the moment, calling him away from the only life he knew.

"Dad, are you ready?" calls his daughter. Is a person ever ready for the word "hospice" to enter one's own vocabulary? Reluctantly, the old man adds another road to the map upon his face. A dying diagnosis will force him to redefine the meaning of his existence.

Effort and productivity slide into the shadows, thus erasing this elderly man's worth. Life seems pointless. Becoming a burden beams rather well into his reality. "*Why?*" he pleads under his shallow breath as he is driven to a room that would unravel his world.

Resting in his recliner from the farm, a stranger appears in the doorway. The old man's heart jolts him awake as this visitor's presence overwhelms him. "Wh... wh-what do you want?" stammers the old man. The strange presence floats across the room with a beacon of brightness. The old man contemplates his sanity as a voice privy to him only speaks.

"Seeds sown must take root before the season ends."

"Well of course seeds have to..." the old man attempts to respond, but the image is gone. Alone in this one room called home, the old man ponders the meaning of his visit. Staring into the silent doorway, a hole in his heart aches for something unknown.

He weeps for the past and he yearns for the future. The old man's presence is filled with turmoil. Shaken by this spirit, he frantically cries out for help. A young lady appears with a tray, permeating the air with tomato soup and grilled cheese. "Time to eat," she cheerfully announces. The old man forgot he hadn't eaten since he arrived. She briskly places the tray on his bedside table and whisks away with a smile.

The old man's focus diverts from the lunch back to his messenger. The words sting his soul like a wasp defending its life. Shoving his soup aside, he senses a starvation within. Impoverished and ignorant of his needs, an answer to his plea arrives.

A third appearance softly walks into his small room. Hunched over a cane, a balding man dressed in a suit politely introduces himself as Jed. "I heard you yelling for help, so I came," he quietly responds.

What could a crippled old guy like himself ever do to help? the old man thought to himself. "Sit down, Jed," he reluctantly offers. The crippled one pulls himself a folding chair and struggles to get comfortable. Jed's crisp blue eyes shine a smile into the old man's anguishing heart. Impressed with his attitude, the old man inquires where he is from.

"I'm in the next room. Been there for ten years," Jed gently replies.

The old man stares at Jed for quite some time. Jed didn't seem to mind. "Jed, how is it you can still smile while confined to one room? Don't you miss your home?"

"Well you see, my friend," Jed calmly states, "my roots are deep as I await for my season to draw near."

The old man gasps. Jed's words beat like a drum to a theme he must learn. "But I don't understand, Jed, I feel useless sitting in here... like cattle awaiting the slaughter." The old man stammers as he chokes back tears.

Jed puts his wrinkled hand upon the old man's shoulder. A warm presence filters from his touch. "There is a seed, a precious seed. Once it is sown into your heart it takes hold and grows deep roots. When the storms of life beat against you, it anchors your soul. Nothing can conquer or defeat one who possesses it. Therefore, I am ready for when the season ends."

The old man soaks in these words like rain on a parched plain. "I believe you are sent to explain the message," he confides.

Jed nods, "I've been praying for you ever since you arrived."

The morning hours have seemingly stretched out to a lifetime. Somehow, time has become a valuable commodity for the old man.

Jed takes a worn-out book from his suit pocket. The tattered pages fall open to John chapter four. Jed puts on his glasses and reads the parable of the sower. The old farmer hangs his head in remorse. "I have been sowing seeds faithfully for the earth's harvest only. My fields have been my world and I ignored the Word that was taught to me as a child." The old man sobs.

Jed leans close to his ear and whispers, "'*Set your affection on things above, not on things on the earth. For you are dead, and your life is hid with Christ in God. Colossians 3:2-3.*' My friend, eternity spent with Jesus far outweighs the regrets of our sins."

The old man looks up, and to his astonishment he sits alone. His tomato soup is cold, but his heart is like a roaring fire.

"Nurse, nurse, please come in!" he calls. Rushing to his room, the young lady who served him soup responds. "Oh nurse, please tell Jed to come back. I have more to ask of him."

The nurse looks startled. "Uh… well. I'm not permitted to share information regarding our residents, but Jed died this morning. How could you even have met him?"

Stunned with disbelief, the old man hushes his sorrow. "Thank-you, nurse. I need to be alone please."

Gazing into space, the old man welcomes the silence. The morning events linger within his mind, creating a longing for more. The peace of God engulfs him like a warm blanket on a winter night. He is ready for the harvest.

A knock on the door intrudes on his thoughts. "Dad, how do you like your new room?"

The old man shakes his head slowly back and forth several times. "Honey, this room has unraveled my world and spun it into something beautiful!"

Shocked at his new attitude, she hands him a package. "I was told to give this to you from an elderly man."

The old man quickly rips it open to find Jed's Bible. A note attached reads, "Sow the precious seed." Tears stream down his crinkly face like rivers on the plowed field. With renewed purpose the old farmer declares, "I now have new fields to prepare!"

> *Then saith he unto his disciples, The harvest truly is plenteous, but the labourers are few; Pray ye therefore the Lord of the harvest, that he will send forth labourers into his harvest. (Matthew 9:37–38)*

Demands of the Day

Keeping up with daily demands wears on our wellness. We wait for our reprieve in various ways, such as recreation or solitude, in order to restore our reserve. Whether you are worn out due to the world's events, work, or grief, there is a never-ending reservoir for you. Why run dry when your demands can dip into a deep pool of pleasure?

Before you file this into the drawer of impossibilities, please read on. Error holds our souls in needless bondage.

> *My People are destroyed from lack of knowledge. (Hosea 4:6)*

Therefore, let's clear up the muddy waters of misconstrued teaching so the truth can free you.

> *And ye shall know the truth, and the truth shall make you free. (John 8:32)*

What is your picture of the Heavenly Father? Unfortunately, many view the Father as legalistic and demanding, making our Lord look unapproachable and unreasonable. However, God demonstrated the desire to be restored in relationship with us by sending Jesus to this earth. He made all provision; we only need to receive His grace. See John 3:16.

Some visualize God as asking people to give up something of worth or not wanting them to partake in pleasure. This attitude portrays the concept, *I have to have fun first before I'm ready to follow Jesus.* We often are confused as to what exactly a good time is. Whatever you are leaping to or from, these "likes" (money, travel, sports, sex, status, career, or relationships) are temporary. Our God is the sustainer of true satisfaction. In fact, He is trying to give what you are designed for: perfect love.

> *And we have known and believed the love that God has for us. God is love, and he who abides in love abides in God, and God in him. (I John 4:16)*

This love may be hard to comprehend, for we are used to people draining us. Add the struggle of loss upon these daily demands and life is immediately off balance. Our Father is more willing to give than we are willing to receive. We know this to be true, for we all have had the experience of looking for love in all the wrong places. Putting Jesus on the pedestal will prove all promises of prosperity hold true. An abundant life only comes through Jesus. The Father is not trying to get something from you; He is running toward you with a heart overflowing with goodness.

> *Such knowledge is too wonderful for me; it is high, I cannot attain unto it. Psalm 139:6*

> *...I am come that they might have life, and that they might have it more abundantly. John 10:10*

Secrets to Silence Insomnia

Have you ever woken up feeling more tossed within than the blankets tangled around you? It is usually in the dark, quiet hours where unresolved issues haunt the heart. Intruders such as grief, guilt, anger, disappointment, fear, or loneliness lead you into war zones rather than granting sweet dreams. Next time your insomnia interrupts your sleep, find solace in a secret dwelling place.

> *He that dwelleth in the secret place of the most High shall abide under the shadow of the Almighty. (Psalm 91:1)*

Jesus, your Savior, awaits in the silence to receive this anguish. Releasing the pressures bottled within will turn the useless hours of struggle into meaningful communion. This, my friend, is an opportune time to listen for the Spirit's mysteries to unfold. Such pleasures await the soul as the Lord works His good pleasures out of your concerns.

> *Having made known unto us the mystery of his will, according to his good pleasure which he hath purposed in himself. Ephesians 1:9*

Allowing the words written through Heavenly inspiration to rest in the hidden chambers of your heart will pull down strongholds. Soon the dawn of morning will arise, casting shadows upon your cares. When deep calls to deep, (Ps. 42:7) treasures are discovered.

> *But God hath revealed them unto us by his Spirit: for the Spirit searcheth all things, yea, the deep things of God. (I Corinthians 2:10)*

> *I will give thee the treasures of darkness, and hidden riches of secret places, that thou mayest know that I, the LORD , which call thee by thy name, am the God of Israel. (Isaiah 45:3)*

One word of revelation from the secret place will straighten the crooked paths in your mind. Whisper the Word you hear into the late hours until He gives you, His beloved, sweet sleep.

> *He revealeth the deep and secret things... (Daniel 2:22)*

When you lie down, you will not be afraid;
When you lie down, your sleep will be sweet.
(Proverbs 3:24)

The Healing Door

An elderly man sat in his truck after the funeral. His vision was blurred by tears begging to fall. Wiping the evidence of weakness away with his sleeve, the old man slowly got out. Staring at the house that held so many memories, he felt numb. Fear found its way into his heart as he gazed upon the front door. Opening the door would mean facing the fact that his wife had died. Dragging his heavy feet into his home, the sorrowful man wandered around in silence. Each room appeared so much larger now that he was alone. With nobody to speak to, he sat on the couch in a daze. The lonely man's heart broke as he peered at his wife's empty chair.

A soft knocking sound broke the silence. Startled, the old man peeked out the window to see who it was. With nobody in view and the sun settling in for the night, the old man figured pure tiredness was playing tricks with his mind.

The thought of sleep was a good plan of escape from his aching heart. Finding his pajamas stuffed in a drawer, he felt an uneasiness in his stomach. Stumbling into the bathroom, he began to perspire in the chilly night. As the old man bent over the sink to splash cool water on his face, he looked at the man in the mirror. Without his wife, the weary man wondered who he was. His life seemed like an erupting volcano about to spew lava into space. The water couldn't cool the steaming unrest bursting within his soul.

Another knock interrupted his emerging anger. Drying his face, the old man shouted into the towel, "Leave me alone!" Shuffling into the bedroom, he laid down into a sinking depression. As the distressed man went to shut off the light, he noticed his wife's Bible. A longing for her presence overwhelmed him. Oh, how she loved spending time with Jesus, he reminisced. Opening the sacred book, he found a verse highlighted in yellow:

> *Ask, and it shall be given you; seek, and ye shall find: knock, and it shall be opened unto you. (Matthew 7:7)*

The knocking he previously heard returned. Listening carefully, the elderly man somehow knew it was a heavenly invitation. Strange but serene, the old man was drawn to read more. Something very satisfying was occurring within his spirit. It was like an orchestra composing an amazing symphony. The words he read soothed his shaken soul as the Holy Spirit opened the door of his heart. The old man found himself very moved to respond to the unseen presence.

> *Behold, I stand at the door, and knock: if any man hear my voice, and open the door, I will come in to him, and will sup with him, and he with me. (Revelation 3:20)*

Behind closed doors, the man's devoted wife prayed daily for his salvation. Her life glowed with an intriguing and attractive persona. She faithfully shared how God imparted grace for every situation. The old man did not quite grasp the meaning of grace until tonight. Supernatural understanding flooded into his entire being. What happened next brought sweet love songs into his soul. The Holy Spirit ushered grief out of his heart as Jesus was welcomed in.

The old man's house no longer appeared empty or lonely. He spent his time reading his wife's Bible and listening to Jesus. Grief no longer lived in the rooms of the man's heart.

> *Blessed is the man that heareth me, watching daily at my gates, waiting at the posts of my doors. (Proverbs 8:34)*

The Hands of Comfort

The clock holds a hollow face, reminding you that time moves on. Its hands march forward without consideration of your aching heart, which yearns to go back where loving arms embraced. During the day your mind moves in slow motion, but it races into the night. Insomnia dominates and demands the energy you need for the morning. In your silent night you plead prayers for comfort.

You know the Father holds your loved one in heaven, but it doesn't dismiss the suffering your earthbound soul endures. The memories of the past haunt your heart. While your precious one was dying, you demanded a miracle. Why, even Lazarus was resurrected. You did not doubt God's almighty power. But the answer was not in the unwrapping of grave clothes, but dressing your loved one with heavenly garments.

Questions swirl within your mind. Can you continue on without your loved one? Your hope hovers dimly beneath the layers of pain. Unwilling to wrap your mind with depression, you open the Book of Life. It speaks a timely message:

A bruised reed shall he not break, and the smoking flax shall he not quench: he shall bring forth judgment unto truth. Isaiah 42:3

Yes, loss has wounded your heart, but it doesn't have to remain broken. How can you be sure? When Jesus was on the cross, He broke His heart for yours. It was here that sorrow faced truth and was brought forth to judgment. He now binds up your broken heart. See Isaiah 61:1. So now ask yourself, where is grief's reign? Certainly not with the risen Lord, nor with you! Therefore, ponder not upon your wounds where grief pounds its pain, and resist waiting for time to heal your pain. Believe the truth: Jesus comforts you from the right hand of God.

If ye then be risen with Christ, seek those things which are above, where Christ sitteth on the right hand of God. (Colossians 3:1)

Faith, Not Fault

Blaming is a common response while grieving. It is considered a defense mechanism. Too fearful to face the facts, the suffering person's pain is diverted into another direction. Usually the pain is projected upon another person. Blaming creates a chasm within as well as without. Unresolved feelings will not lead to resolution. Complicating matters further, if the blame is cast unto God, a blind spot is carved into the heart. In the dark cave of distress, it would be beneficial to receive the comfort of one who not only cares, but who can also lift you out.

> *The Lord is my light and salvation; whom shall I fear? The Lord is the strength of my life of whom shall I be afraid? (Psalm 27:1)*

Rather than find fault with the Father, have faith in His love. People who blame God need to get better acquainted with Him. Their perspective is skewed as they point fingers at the wrong source. The Father did not orchestrate this death, nor designate the grief imposed upon you. Sin and the powers of darkness rule in this realm—not our Lord.

> *For we wrestle not against flesh and blood, but against principalities, against powers, against the rulers of the darkness of this world, against spiritual wickedness in high places. (Ephesians 6:12)*

Convert these accusations into trust. Trust is developed through knowing someone well; a deepening of one's relationship. Grief is the opportune time to quiet the offenses. Do not fear the searing sensation of sadness that is trying to surface. Sip from the soul-refreshing Scriptures. The Holy Spirit will dismiss your fears, cleanse your thoughts, and operate on your wounds.

> *For the Word of God is quick, and powerful, and sharper than any two-edged sword, piercing even to the dividing asunder of soul and spirit, and of the joints and marrow, and is a discerner of the thoughts and intent of the heart. (Hebrews 4:1)2*

All this is possible because the true blame of sin was cast onto the innocent Son of God. Your Father has wounded His Son to banish the principalities empowering sorrow. Your dark fears wrapped in the cave of grief now face the light of God's healing grace.

Rejoice not against me, O mine enemy: when I fall, I shall arise; when I sit in darkness, the Lord shall be a light unto me. (Micah 7:8)

Shackled in Sorrow

If you think the good ol' days are waving goodbye to a hopeful future, you've been captivated by the punishing lies of loss. Wondering why you are left behind creates discomfort while blurring your faith. Before your past overturns your purpose, understand how these signs of grief won't point you in the right direction.

Without warning, the symptoms of sorrow may immobilize your motivation. Feeling as though life is over because love has left your side can misconstrue God's plan. Such a belief stems from an erroneous view of love's relationship with sorrow. Too often, sorrow is treated as a symbol of love. Love and grief are not companions in the Kingdom of God. If they were friends, Jesus would have invited sorrow to follow Him into Heaven. However, Jesus shut the gate on grief because loss is death's soulmate.

Therefore, refuse to serve the sentence of grief when freedom was purchased for you. Jesus released you from the unseen chains binding you into bereavement. Breaking the link to loss begins with looking through the eyes of Christ. As enlightenment from Scripture is received, inspiration will replenish your desire to live again.

> *The Spirit of the Lord is upon me, because he hath anointed me to preach the gospel to the poor; he hath sent me to heal the broken-hearted, to preach deliverance to the captives and recovery of sight to the blind, to set at liberty them that are bruised. (Luke 4:18)*

When revelation unfolds, you will no longer accept death's dusty rags of depression. After all, Our Lord Jesus isn't wearing the garments of the past, and nor should you.

Rather than cozy up with grief, put on garments which free you from the spirit of heaviness. When reminiscing tries to handcuff your hope, recall the truth. You can love someone who has passed from this world without wearing sorrow's shackles. Peer into the pages of Scripture; inspiration of praise will flow over your mournful memories.

> *To appoint to those who mourn in Zion, to give to them a garland for ashes, the oil of joy for mourning, the garment of praise for the spirit of heaviness; that they may be called trees of righteousness, the planting of Yahweh, that he may be glorified. (Isaiah 61:3)*

The Word That Carries Sorrow

Strengthened with all might, according to his glorious power, unto all patience and longsuffering with joyfulness. (Colossians 1:1)

People struggling with sorrow may stuff their feelings away to avoid unsolicited sympathy. Hearing "I'm so sorry" may come across to the discouraged as if they are to be pitied. There are no perfect words to say to a person suffering from loss. One word may work for one while offending another. What does one say at a sensitive time as such?

Generally, people who are downcast are conscientious about looking put together and strong. Therefore, common complaints from the bereaved include the unwelcome crying and sporadic mood swings. It is embarrassing when tears don't respect the locks on the heart. Instead, a song, scent, or sight can solicit keys to open emotional doors. While in bereavement, people wonder why they don't feel like themselves and set tall expectations impossible to achieve.

Step alongside the weary pilgrim to provide permission to simply be. The right word is the presence of the Word; Jesus, our Lord. *The Word was God (John 1:1).* Allow your prayers and His wisdom to guide you as you reach out to help. Being with those who suffer is more important than what you say.

The good word is that grace overturns grief. Grief doesn't have to stay buried in secret spaces, wearing one down, when Jesus offers resurrected strength. The Father has put Him to grief to remove its power over His people. Jesus carried sorrow so it wouldn't remain in a saddened heart.

The Voice

Grief makes noise. It is like dynamite exploding all peace out of your heart. You either cry softly or shout angrily when it shatters your life. When grief claims the ground in your soul, you seek to understand what has happened and search for someone who will listen. People don't know how you long to speak about YOUR grief without interruption. We all know people who start out with a listening ear, but interject their own story on how grief has hurt them. It just ruins your moment and you are left hanging onto this boulder.

Finding a friend who has more ears than mouth will help roll the grief off the cliff of your shoulders. Your heaviness can be lifted, at least for a while. Unfortunately, in the quietness of your home, the boulder comes rolling back. Why has it returned? You feel crushed when you look back to that moment of relief. Just when hope extended a foot forward, grief pushed you back. You press on in your own valley where grief echoes defeat.

Grief is also hectic. There is an endless list of things to do—without warning, funeral preparations, thank-you cards, phone calls, estate plans, and other unforeseen tasks barge rudely into your life. The first few months are a blur as your adrenaline pushes you on. Exhaustion chases you down and your feelings are somewhere in space. Your voice has been buried under the burden of busyness. Giving up as you get more and more lost in the wilderness of lamentation, you seek deliverance. This time your voice is heard from the divine.

> *Thou callest in trouble, and I delivered thee; I answered thee in the secret place of thunder... (Psalms 81:7)*

Unbeknownst to you, a voice was whispering in the midst of your clatter. You stop to listen. The shaking in your heart is quieted by the still small voice of God.

> *And after the earthquake a fire; but the Lord was not in the fire: and after the fire a still small voice. (I Kings 19:12)*

Opening your soul to the Word of God ushers in much needful peace. The blasting noise is replaced with harmony. Your heart remains still; grief has heard the voice of God.

> *Peace, peace to him that is far off, and to him that is near, saith the LORD; and I will heal him. (Isaiah 57:19)*

Sorrow Blends into the Sunrise

The spirit of a soul slips off silently as sounds of sorrow fill the air. A life wisps away while those remaining sit stunned in grief, the immediate surroundings suddenly look so different. Has someone removed the color? Black and white splatter the room. Sadness sifts through the events at hand. It is difficult to see life as before. The view is narrowed as mourning presses its suffering into sight. Lost is the way out of the pain—yours, that is. The beloved lies peacefully still, displaying there's so much more. Departed from thy side, the search begins.

Pondering the past yields little productivity. Frustrated with the facts, a surge of strength forges forward. Anger subsides into a subtle Selah. Heaven sends a rainbow while handfuls of hope flicker into the horizon. The transformation was effortless. While puzzled and pleased, the grace of God begins painting a new story. Eager to participate, sorrow blends into the sunrise.

Grief's paintbrush has put its stripes on Jesus. The cross has transitioned darkness into a glorious light. Your heart receives understanding. The signature of the Savior's finished work personally invites, and the entrance into eternity ends your search.

> *The eyes of your understanding being enlightened; that ye may know what is the hope of his calling, and what the riches of the glory of his inheritance in the saints. (Ephesians 1:18)*

The Question of Why

When grief blasts through your heart, a string of questions can strangle your mind. What happened? Who is to blame? Where do I go? How do I cope? It isn't out of the ordinary that you need to assemble your disassembled life. And yet, there may be one particular question that squeezes out your peace more than the rest: the haunting question of *why?*

Asking why may be an attempt to attach meaning to your situation or to simulate a sense of control over your pain. Regardless of the underlying reason, the confusion mixed within this question wars against your peace. Although not all answers are found, resolution is near when you turn your whys over to the cross. Come and see, it is where Jesus Himself asked the Father…

My God, My God ***why*** *hast thou forsaken me? (Mark 15:34) (Emphasis mine)*

Jesus asked 'why' in the midst of His grief also. He was severed from the Father's love. This grief was darker than we could ever imagine. If you think about it, when your loved one died, you were not cut off from the *source* of love. Not so with Jesus; He was banned completely from the Father. It was so because of our sins.

As Jesus bore the sins of the world on the cross, He was expelled from His Father. Sin cannot reside in the presence of perfect love. They are polar opposites. Sin includes death and God involves life. Sin includes grief and God involves peace. Everything good is derived from the Father and every destructive power stems from sin. Sin is destroyed in the presence of God. Therefore, only goodness can enter the kingdom of God.

It is a relief to know that our Father did not want us to be eternally banished from Himself. This is why Jesus paid the price for our sins: so we could be with the Father. God is obviously good, so why are people blaming Him for the bad that occurs in their lives?

This one question can answer one more: *why your loved one had to die.* God did not cause death, nor the grief it created. Rather, your Father delivered you from sin, death, and grief. He did not deem it upon you. Turn to the truth, where answers will reply to your why.

> *God so loved the world that he gave His only begotten son, that whosoever believeth in Him shall not perish, but have everlasting life. (John 3:16)*

What A Waste or Waist: The War with Food

Finding an empty chair at the table is one of the most dreaded experiences after the death of a loved one. After all, eating is a social time where conversation is prominent over the passing of aroma-filled dishes. Eating alone accentuates the truth; there is no one to share your laughter or life.

Frequently, grieving people say that food loses its taste. It seems to be a bother to bring out all those ingredients to make a meal for one person. No wonder your energy is gone. The fuel that once flattered the plate with fancy delicacies is now kept hidden in refrigerators and cupboards.

OR

Food becomes the focus of your day. Chocolate or chips attempt to fill the absence of the hand once held. Comfort food loses its title when the brief encounter displays more dissatisfaction on the scale.

Famine or feast, food ignites an internal war when grief arrives. Whether you are wasting away to skin and bone or welcoming inches to your waistline, the stress of loss needs soothing. Through efforts of your own, you discover it is not found on a menu of your own making.

Remove your focus off of your appetite and look on to the Lord Jesus Christ, who offers you the bread of life. He will lavish your grief with comfort, satisfying the empty space no one but He can fill.

> *Blessed be God, even the Father of our Lord Jesus Christ, the Father of mercies, and the God of all comfort. (2 Corinthians 1:3)*

> *For the LORD shall comfort Zion: he will comfort all her waste places; and he will make her wilderness like Eden, and her desert like the garden of the LORD; joy and gladness shall be found therein, thanksgiving, and the voice of melody. (Isaiah. 51:3)*

God is willing to make your soul's desert into a delicious dessert. He is the peace for your barren pantry. Open the door of your heart and accept the invitation to His table. The Words on His menu will not disappoint. They read:

> *I will not leave you comfortless: I will come to you. (John 14:18)*

Fix a place setting for Jesus, and mealtime will take on a whole different meaning.

Disturbing Thorns

Remember the word unto thy servant, upon which thou hast caused me to hope. This is my comfort in my affliction: for thy word hath quickened me. The proud have had me greatly in derision: yet have I not declined from thy law. I remembered thy judgments of old, O Lord; and have comforted myself. (Psalm 119:49–52)

When battling grief, the soul is vulnerable. People rub you the wrong way. They can easily get under your skin. You surely don't need a double dose of pain poking into your heart. When conflict happens, it is good to be on God's side, where healing (not harm) occurs. Rather than giving in to your feelings and the grievance, receive God's grace, which keeps you in peace. While these uncomfortable encounters jab pain into your soul, there is a better plan than to get caught up in the conflict.

First of all, know your position in this world. There are two kingdoms co-existing in your midst: the Father's and Satan's. As a child of the Father, you are born into His kingdom. This means you have the Holy Spirit equipping you with His protective shield.

> *My goodness, and my fortress; my high tower, and my deliverer; my shield, and he in whom I trust; who subdueth my people under me. (Psalm 144:2)*

The shield is His Spirit of love, peace, joy, mercy, forgiveness, faith, and hope. Whatever encompasses the Father makes up His shield. Therefore, remaining in Christ prevents Satan from penetrating into your heart. The only way the wicked one can hurt you is by tempting you to sin. If you respond to the spirit of dissention (who lies behind your contender) with hate and harm, he finds a portal to provoke you. However, this is where it is vital to know provision for victory is already available. Your Father gives you grace for these afflictions.

> *And lest I should be exalted above measure through the abundance of the revelations, there was given to me a thorn in the flesh, the messenger of Satan to buffet me, lest I should be exalted above measure. For this thing I besought the Lord thrice, that it*

> *might depart from me. And he said unto me, My grace is sufficient for thee: for my strength is made perfect in weakness. Most gladly therefore will I rather glory in my infirmities, that the power of Christ may rest upon me. Therefore I take pleasure in infirmities, in reproaches, in necessities, in persecutions, in distresses for Christ's sake: for when I am weak, then am I strong. (II Corinthians 12:7-10)*

Avail yourself to receiving God's grace at all times, because thorns won't be removed from your life quite yet. However, grace is your favor in the war. The strength received from God grants you a position of reigning over all wickedness. Therefore, soak yourself into God's Word, which extinguishes the arrows coming toward you. The truth will guard your mind from engaging into the other kingdom. Rest in your refuge; Jesus will be your shield.

> *Above all, taking the shield of faith; wherewith ye shall be able to quench all the fiery darts of the wicked. (Ephesians 6:16)*

One day these thorns will be removed. Due to the Father's long suffering, patience, and love for all people (including those who are causing you pain), He will not destroy them. He is giving every opportunity for them to receive Him. Your prayers for the people who hold the thorns may prevent them from being burned in the lake of fire.

> *But I say unto you, Love your enemies, bless them that curse you, do good to them that hate you, and pray for them which despitefully use you, and persecute you. (Matthew 5:44)*

Until the close of the age, stay in peace where Jesus holds His position for your protection. This is where you also will reign, in the kingdom where the Father's kindness prevails.

Creating A Cocoon

Have you felt like avoiding people? What about darting down another aisle of the grocery store when a familiar face is driving the oncoming shopping cart? Grief can cause you to react in ways you never imagined. But think about it: you haven't felt so raw, exposed, or sensitive before the death of your beloved either. Things have changed, and you may think people you know are also acting differently.

The familiar voices you once welcomed into your life now seem to be pouring out pitiful responses. One more comment is too much for your heart to handle. Have their loving eyes really changed into scrutinizing stares? Grief is driving you into isolation. Worn out from the world, you begin constructing a cocoon. Being home alone and allowing no one into your personal space suits you just fine. No worries, you don't need a psychiatrist. It is quite natural to prefer protection over the possibility of one more painful attack.

Grieving people usually feel vulnerable and misunderstood. Thinking nobody grasps what they are going through, they feel safer alone. Guards go up without thought. While grieving walls keep people out, they are also keeping the pain within. The shelter is a much-needed resort for reflection. After some time, truth sets in: life in a cocoon is really not working.

If this sounds like you, please realize you can't survive living within your self-made walls. Cocoons are temporary shelters, and even insects know they eventually must escape them. It may be hard to believe there is a new life outside of your grief. Coming out may seem so very scary. My recommendation: don't do it alone.

The courage to shed your cocoon casing is only possible in the presence of someone you value and trust. In your midst, there is one who is willing to unwrap the threads of grief strangling your heart and release you into the presence of divine freedom.

> *...he hath sent me to bind up the broken-hearted, to proclaim liberty to the captives, and the opening of the prison to them that are bound. (Isaiah 61:1)*

Are you ready to come out and allow Jesus to transform your hurt into health and wholeness?

Jesus will remove your pain and pour gladness into its place. *Thou hast turned for me my mourning into dancing: thou hast put off my sackcloth, and girded me with gladness. (Ps. 30:11)*

He will give your weariness, wings and strength. *But they that wait upon the LORD shall renew their strength;*

they shall mount up with wings like eagles; they shall run, and not be weary, and they shall walk, and not faint. (Is. 40:31)

Jesus will shield you. *Every word of God is pure: he is a shield to those who put their trust in him. (Prov. 30:5)*

He will carry you when your heart is faint. *He shall feed his flock like a shepherd: he shall gather the lambs with his arm, and carry them in his bosom, and shall gently lead those that are with young. (Is. 40:11)*

Jesus has all your wants and needs covered. *The LORD is my shepherd, I shall not want (Ps. 23:1)*

He is true to His Word; trust Him with your way out of grief. *Commit thy way unto the LORD; trust also in him; and he shall bring it to pass. (Ps. 37:5)*

Walk outside of your shelter with the one who will love you back to life. Your fear will fade into the presence of His perfect peace. *There is no fear in love; but perfect love casteth out fear, because fear hath torment. (I John 4:18)*

It is safe *to* come out of your cocoon to a life beyond your grief. Christ will bring comfort to your heart like a garden where butterflies soar and songs of praise reside.

> *For the LORD shall comfort Zion: he will comfort all her waste places; and he will make her wilderness like Eden, and her desert like the garden of the LORD; joy and gladness shall be found therein,*

thanksgiving, and the voice of melody. (Isaiah 51:3)

I, even I am he that comforteth you: who art thou, that thou shouldest be afraid of a man that shall die, and of the son of man which shall be made as grass. (Isaiah 51:12)

Alone, but Not Lonely

"Good grief!" Do you recall this infamous expression from Charlie Brown? He often found himself in depressing situations. It is quite an oxymoron; what good can one find in grief? Grief grabs your heart, tears it open, and leaves it with gaping loneliness. If you don't know what to do with the empty space it creates, you are not alone. Loneliness is a chief complaint and challenge for anyone who is adjusting to a significant loss.

Anticipating invitations for the holidays, special occasions, or Sunday afternoons may be especially dreaded. There is an awkwardness of fitting in with people who continue to smile while you shelter the gnawing ache within. Avoiding people only isolates you more, but standing in a crowd accentuates you are alone. What do you do with this hole that grief has rudely bore, offering no help to fill it in?

Begin by looking past all the people. They do not possess the ability to fill up the pockets in your heart. The love you had enjoyed was really derived from a deeper source: your Savior. It is easy to lose sight of your first love, Jesus, when facing the loss of a loved one, but He doesn't lose sight of you. You lay heavy on his mind. Jesus woos your weary soul as you wander aimlessly amidst the crowds.

Dare to be by yourself. Alone doesn't mean lonely. Listen for the invitation to dine with the living bread. Jesus satisfies your hungering heart like no other. Partaking at His table will fill your hollow space.

Won't you entrust the Lord with your loneliness? The ache will be answered when your heart strings are drawn into His loving embrace.

> *The LORD hath appeared of old unto me, and saying, Yea, I have loved thee with an everlasting love: therefore with lovingkindness have I drawn thee. (Jeremiah 31:3)*

Falling Behind with Grief, or Moving Forward with God

Fall is a time of both beauty and loss. The brilliant leaves we all wait to admire will release from their branches only to crunch beneath our feet. Barren trees will be left staring down at what was once a beautiful part of their lives.

Grief can be likened to the autumn season. There are wonderful memories coloring our lives while the empty spot at the table reminds our hearts death has made a visit. How to move on without your loved one is a question often asked. Most people don't want to even talk about moving forward. This term feels dishonoring and disconnecting from the one who has died. Change is hard for most people. Familiarity breeds security. It may seem more acceptable to be in step with this season's time change, instructing you to turn back the hands of time, rather than spring ahead into life.

If you have experienced a loss, you may feel you are navigating just fine one day only to find yourself falling backward the next. With the stress of adjusting to numerous changes, mourning won't cooperate with your planner. Forgetfulness and futility surrender to sorrow.

While there are layers of reasons which hinder the healing process, one pertinent factor consider is looking back. Don't be misled—ruminating over the past has its time and purpose, but it is unhelpful to *remain* on memory lane. People who only focus on death and loss will bump into their future. Giving yourself permission to participate in today's activities as well as to plan for tomorrow is perfectly acceptable and advised. Your loved one would want you to keep on living, and so does your Heavenly Father. New opportunities are being created and you are designed to fulfill them.

> *Remember ye not the former things, neither consider the things of old. Behold, I will do a new thing; now it shall spring forth; shall ye not know it? I will even make a way in the wilderness and rivers in the desert. (Isaiah 43:18–19)*

You can't make a difference living in the past. Allow memories to be served on a love platter, not on the chopping board of loss. Jesus is in your tomorrows, so do not fear. He is in your past, so be thankful. The future is filled with His hope; so proceed forward.

For I know the thoughts that I think toward you, saith the LORD, thoughts of peace, and not of evil, to give you an expected end. (Jeremiah 29:11)

The Cup

Grief is like walking through a desert. The start of the trip goes quite well. No exhaustion or discouragement has appeared as you venture out, filled with adrenaline and drive. Initially, after a loss, the demands of the day call for your full attention. Your focus is on getting through the paperwork and funeral. This leaves little time to tend to your personal needs. However, when the effects of grief can't hide in your knapsack any longer, you realize you're not functioning as well as you thought.

The walk through the desert begins to bring some irritation. The sun gets hotter, and you notice little things are bothering you. There is no shade; your companion talks too much; your water bottle is warm. You begin to lose your drive. So it is with grief. New feelings and responses remind you there is more to contend with than the list of duties on your desk. What used to take minutes to accomplish now drags on like a tortoise finding water. The lack of clarity angers you. You question why you can't stream through life in your usual manner. The next segment of your journey is quite humbling.

Midway through the first year of grief, reality sinks in. Life events accentuate the absence of your loved one. Your water bottle is near empty and your energy battles the sudden wind storm of feelings. Out of nowhere, the sorrow whips you down and your tears flow without warning. You begin to re-examine your strength and stability. Questions of weakness creep into your parched mind, carving doubt into your character. Your thirst for relief from this walk with grief is finally admitted. Now you begin to look for an oasis.

Thirst is a driver. It can drive people to satisfy dehydration with water or it can drive people to numb feelings through other substances. The cup we choose can result in restoration or destruction. When the stress of grief pours over your peace, receive the cup that saved you from this suffering.

The Cup of Suffering

There is a cup which contains all the suffering of the world. It is called the cup of wrath. It was consumed by our Savior, who had a choice to pick it up or allow it to pass. Within this cup was all the sin that separated you and I from our Heavenly Father. Imagine drinking in murder, guilt, grief, disease, abuse, shame etc. This, my friend, was not an ordinary choice. Think about it—we drink to relieve suffering, not to welcome it. However, if it wasn't for this cup, we would be destined to destruction. Either Jesus drinks it for us or we would be removed from our Heavenly Father's presence forever.

Jesus knew the walk before Him was going to be more than stressful. He felt the pressure to take the suffering of the world upon Himself. This punishment was to be ours and not His to deserve. It was real, and Jesus had a choice. We hear the anguish in His words as Jesus cried out:

> And he went a little further, and fell on his face, and prayed, saying, *O my Father, if it be possible, let this cup pass from me: nevertheless not as I will, but as thou wilt. (Matthew 26:39)*

He chose the Father's will. Why? Because Jesus knew it would be the end of your grief. Your walk in the desert would be over. He looked at the Father's heart and beheld your face. The thirst for justice drove Him to drink in the wrath of punishment for the sins of the world, including yours. Jesus looked past the cup of suffering onto the cup He could offer you today. A new cup that saved you from your sorrow.

The Cup of Salvation

This new cup freely offered does not include the suffering that Jesus partook of. It has living waters filled with salvation. We think salvation is reserved only for afterlife. Although that is a huge aspect of it, this cup is also meant to satisfy your thirst today. After all, it is now that you need help; heaven doesn't have broken hearts. You are saved from sin, death, and yes—also from grief.

Jesus demonstrated this truth to a thirsty woman getting a drink at a well. He did not say to her, "When you enter heaven your thirst will be satisfied." Instead, Jesus invited her to partake of His cup. This new cup would meet her needs from that moment on right into eternity. You see, Jesus was offering her a relationship with Himself.

> *But whosoever drinketh of the water that I shall give him shall never thirst; but the water that I shall give him shall be in him a well of water springing up into everlasting life. (John 4:14)*

What a refreshing way to walk through the desert of grief! Journey with Jesus, who willingly gives you restoration. No need to feel ashamed of your weakness; He understands how you feel because He went through this grief for you. Rest assured, when grievous times want to fill your cup, you can turn it over and receive from His cup instead. Why not drink from a cup that will never run dry? Your cup won't be half empty or half full, but overflowing!

...my cup runneth over. (Psalm 23:5)

Job Receives the Gift of Grace

As we page through the Scriptures, we ponder the path of one who possessed great wealth, earned the respect of the community, and cherished his family. One day Satan roamed the heavens requesting to wipe away all this man possessed; for Satan said it is only for blessings this man is faithful. The Lord allowed the test, but put limits upon his life. Satan could wipe out all this man had, but could not kill him. Tragedy soon after struck like the winds of a hurricane, thrashing away his family and livelihood. This man desperately cried out to the Father as he rode the tumultuous waves of grief.

The faithful soul, Job, had lost his livelihood, daughters, and sons, only to be engulfed with boils blistering his body. History hangs a banner for his great patience. It was exhibited with the candid critic of his wife, who ordered him to curse God and die. Job's tolerance also stretched toward his well-meaning friends, who tossed unhelpful counsel his way. With much misery, Job continued to seek God while he was greatly misunderstood.

Job denied not his affliction nor his misfortune. He was honest and honorable as he tried to understand his painful journey. Job held no embarrassment for his emotional distress. He described his grief as weighing heavier than the sand of the sea (see Job 6: 2 -3). Loathing life itself, Job wanted to be left alone and cursed the day of his birth. He had reached his limits. Job's emotions were well acquainted with the depths of darkness. However, as he was tormented in the trenches of sorrow, he felt his pious ways should only bring good promise.

Job built a case before God and his friends, defending his purity. How could his righteous life deserve such wrath? Linking his loss to his deeds was not what this was about; Job soon would understand.

While grief relentlessly splattered his life, the heavenly Father was anchoring him in the storm. Job continued to worship God while the winds of grief whipped through his strength. However, Job stood firm on the stand against grief, upholding the evidence of his good works. When he concluded his dissertation of defense, Job eventually saw a light beyond his distress. The Father revealed the error of Job's ways.

As God was introducing Himself on a personal level, Job's perspective was put correctly into place (see Job 40-41). God concludes His speech by saying,

> *He beholdeth all high things: he is king over all the children of pride. (Job 41:34)*

Job then cried in dust and ashes, no longer over his loss, but for his pride. He was humbled yet free. Job no longer upheld merit in his own righteous deeds, but understood it was within God's power to freely bestow all blessings. Job repented as God's grace opened his eyes.

> *I have heard of thee by the hearing of the ear: but now mine eye seeth thee. (Job 42:5)*

When Job changed his mind on the matters of God, he forgave his friends for their unhelpful advice. God's grace showered again; replacing Job's loss with double.

> *And the LORD turned the captivity of Job, when he prayed for his friends: also the LORD gave Job twice as much as he had before. (Job 42:10)*

Job, who only heard about God, finally received spiritual eyes to know Him. Job realized his own works were tossed out of the courtroom for any goodness he tried to present. Job held no power over God. Kindness came his way because of God's grace. Job received double for his loss. Does not Job's story share a message for all who mourn?

If you are struggling with sorrow, take heart; our gracious God will bring restoration. When the thief of grief robs your joy and peace, join Job and rejoice in the redeemer who lives, gives, and restores.

For your shame ye shall have double; and for confusion they shall rejoice in their portion: therefore in their land they shall possess the double: everlasting joy shall be unto them. (Isaiah 61:7)

Grief Grew in a Garden but Died on Its Tree

There once was a garden filled with flowers and fruit
that birthed our Father's dream.
Fashioned with care for a family to share, His love
would forever beam.
A deceitful temptation from a devil nearby, drew them
away from the love they knew.
The garden was saddened, for barren it was and weeds
came where flowers once grew.
Angels stood guard with swords at the gate, for within
death did hold all of their fate.
The trees failed to shadow the shattering shame,
Adam and Eve were only to blame.
Creation groaned when grief entered in, looking for
God to end all the sin.
As death and grief roamed to and fro, the Father's Son
would take their blow.
The garden did offer a tree that was dead, where Jesus
held power to crush Satan's head.
Healing is offered, by grace you are saved, death and
its grief have no grip on the grave.

Jesus paid the price for your loss, so receive His peace gained at the cross.
Enter the Kingdom where life is restored, but leave grief at the gate; it can't enter this door.

Enter ye in at the strait gate, for wide is the gate, and broad is the way that leadeth to destruction, and many there be which go in thereat: Because strait is the gate, and narrow is the way, which leadeth unto life, and few there be that find it. (Matthew 7:13–14)

The Plague of Grief

What is afflicting your soul today can affect your tomorrow. Grief unattended is a serious condition. Ignoring pain creates problems in your body, mind, and emotions. Whether it is sickness, disease, confusion, depression, lack of motivation, or appetite changes, the manifestation of a mournful heart goes on and on. Devastation due to divorce, death, loss of a limb, job, or dignity creates a portal for a plague to pummel away your peace. It is quite evident: grief is not your friend, but a foe to your well-being. If sorrow was meant to coexist in your life, why do hospitals hire grief therapists and chaplains to assist in relieving it? Grief is a national healthcare concern, as well as yours, because it causes intense suffering.

Although a grieving heart is slowly being recognized as a root cause for other ailments, it still lacks social acceptance. Therefore, many people are not willing to admit to this pain and choose to deny its existence. As with any stressful condition, covering it up complicates finding a cure. This is why choosing a trustworthy confidant capable of curing grief is highly recommended. If you wonder who can be trusted with your broken heart, take advice from a wise man who lived long ago.

Solomon, a well-versed soul, was blessed with more wisdom than any other human. Solomon brought the problems plaguing God's people to the holy temple. Scripture doesn't record him developing a five-step plan on pain management or recommending a new self-help book; instead, Solomon turned to the almighty God who had power to heal all conditions.

> *What prayer and supplication soever be made by any man, or by all thy people Israel, which shall know every man* ***the plague of his own heart,*** *and spread forth his hands toward this house; Then hear thou in heaven thy dwelling place, and forgive...* (I Kings 8:38 -39) (Emphasis mine)

As you read the Old Testament, please remember there is nothing out of date when it comes to the Father rescuing distressed hearts. The difference is in location. The Father isn't limited to brick and mortar to perform His healing services, for His Spirit resides in new temples.

> *What? Know ye not that your body is the temple of the Holy Ghost which is in you, which ye have of God, and ye are not your own? (I Corinthians 6:19)*

When you are the temple for God's Spirit, you surely don't have to wait to attend a church service or go to a clinic to receive healing. While you spend time In His presence, you will find out He has much to say about your sorrow. *Call unto me, and I will answer thee, and shew thee great and mighty things which thou knowest not. (Jer. 33:3*)

Search Scripture and discover His promise of peace is ready to be poured into your aching soul. *Behold, I will bring it health and cure, and I will cure them and will reveal unto them the abundance of peace and truth. (Jer. 33:6)*

You might be questioning the relevance of this promise. Will healing really happen? Doubts usually stem from earthly disappointments or errors of teaching. Trust the Father who speaks truth with power and is able to perform. *Behold, the days come, saith the LORD, that I will perform that good thing which I have promised unto the house of Israel and to the house of Judah. (Jer. 33:14)*

As you look to the Word of promise and wait for your heart to be made whole, it is easy to slip into impatience. In the world of immediate gratification, waiting is not highly valued. No need to be discouraged when answers are not immediate. The timing is in the Father's hands.

Recall how Abraham and Sarah had to wait for the promise of a child. They knew God was faithful in keeping His promise. Their faith was not placed in themselves or outward proof. *Through faith also Sarah herself received strength to conceive seed, and was delivered of a child when she was past age, because* ***she judged him faithful who had promised****. (Heb. 11:11) (Emphasis mine)* Faith in the Father is not a walk-by-sight relationship. His Word implanted in our hearts will guide us. *For we walk by faith, not by sight. (II Cor. 5:7)*

Solomon, Abraham, and Sarah all trusted in God's power to change disappointing situations. Your turn is here. The plan for your plague has already been placed on Jesus Christ. *Yet it pleased the LORD to bruise him; he hath put him to grief… (Is. 53:10)* Your sorrow will be turned into a healing peace as you put your faith in Him.

> *And he said unto her, Daughter, thy faith hath made thee whole; go in peace, and be whole of thy plague. (Mark 5:34)*

> *For he had healed many; insomuch that they pressed upon him for to touch him, as many as had plagues. (Mark 3:10)*

Treasures of Truth

I sought the LORD, and he heard me, and delivered me from all my fears. (Psalm 34:4)

Tossing and turning like a restless sea, your night of expected slumber is unsettled. You thrash your covers aside to surrender to the beast of insomnia. The aroma of fresh brewed coffee offers a dim hope for a jump start on the day. However, the clouds in your mind house darkened memories. The distraction is overpowering, leaving your capacity to function paralyzed. Longing for crisp clarity to focus on your crowded calendar, you sob with regret to accomplish a simple task. Engulfed in feelings of despair, an added burden of going crazy is birthed.

Pushing aside your schedule, a call to your counselor takes precedence. Another therapy session of dumping your problems onto the desk of expertise. Volumes of books surround the therapist's office. Unfortunately, hope and relief remain outside their pages. Within a few hours after the session, the haunting ghosts return to torment anyway.

In the private chambers of your home, you cry out to the unseen counselor. An ancient book on your shelf, the Bible, now finds your fingers paging for an answer.

> *If I say, Surely the darkness shall cover me; even the night shall be light about me. Yea, the darkness hideth not from thee; but the night shineth as the day: the darkness and the light are both alike to thee. (Psalm 139:11–12)*

A warm presence softens your heart. The Heavenly Father's Word unveils hidden treasures. Gifts wrapped in grace are now presented.

> *I will give thee the* ***treasures*** *of* ***darkness****, and hidden riches of secret places, that you may know that it is I, the LORD, which call thee by thy name, am the God of Israel. (Isaiah 45:3) (Emphasis mine)*

We all love treasures! Precious commodities are so sacred and safely kept. Inspiration to dig further into Scripture surges in you. Faithful is the Father! The next verse sings freedom that no counselor has ever shared before.

> *There is therefore now no condemnation to them which are in Christ Jesus who walk not after the flesh, but after the Spirit. (Romans 8:1)*

Suddenly, you discover it is condemnation keeping you in depression. The thought that you were not over your grief soon enough instantly dissipates. Regret that you didn't stay home the day your loved one died miraculously disappears. Wishing you would have said "I love you" more washes away. Looking back at what was left undone is covered by love.

Jesus declared, *it is finished (John 19:30).* Every thought of persecution ceases.

How Long, Lord?

Maybe your fiery trial is best described as a forest fire. You may gaze at its flames, which have no end in sight, and doubt if there is an escape plan. Have you reached a point where you ran out of hope? This is actually a perfect place to be. Why? You can stop any self-reliance from creeping in. Dependence is the position to be in to receive even more provision from Jesus!

It is easy to shift from leaning on Jesus to working frantically against grief within your own strength. When you detect your energy looks more like the warning light of low fuel on your car, it is time to get off the road of self-sufficiency. Jesus will graciously give you more reserve.

Since the Father gives you everything you need to endure your trial, there is nothing to dread when it comes your way. Think of it this way: you are privileged to participate in these types of situations, because trials are the altar where God proves His power.

Fire: Evidence of God's Power

A great witness of God's power is in I Kings 18. Elijah had a showdown with followers of Baal as to prove who God Almighty really is. Elijah was used in this miraculous event when the fire of God consumed the sacrifice even after it was doused with water.

> *Then the fire of the LORD fell, and consumed the burnt sacrifice, and the wood, and the stones, and the dust, and licked up the water that was in the trench. (I Kings 18:38)*

God will show up for you when you are under the pressure of grief. So, rather than get all wrapped up in your painful symptoms, learn from Elijah, who kept his mind on the One who will prove His faithfulness. Jesus will dry your tears like Elijah's soaking sacrifice.

The Grace Side of Grief

When the trial of grief tries to push you down, remember you are on the grace side of grief. Jesus consumed sorrow's power, allowing you to receive the joy and comfort He victoriously won through the cross. Declare your healing as the trial proves Jesus is Lord over grief.

Keep Focused

Mine eye also is dim by reason of sorrow, and all my members are as a shadow. (Job 17:7)

Walking into the bright outdoors from a dark room certainly affects your vision. It takes a while for your eyes to adjust. So it is with grief—it can impact your vision. Living in the light of your loved one's presence one moment and facing the dark world of grief alone can be frightening. It may surprise you, but this changing experience doesn't have to be filled with gloom and doom. The secret? Fix your eyes on Jesus.

Keeping your eyes on the light of Christ will keep you from stumbling in the dark corners of grief. You don't have to walk into this new circumstance alone. Jesus is here. Jesus met the darkness of grief so you can adjust to your loss through His empowering healing grace.

How can Jesus help you adjust? It began when He was banned from the presence of the source of all our love. You see, Jesus lost connection with the Father when He took our sins to the cross. Jesus could not see the Father when sin, death, and grief separated Him from divine perfection.

This was the most horrific grief ever known. Three hours of unnatural darkness hovered upon the world when Jesus hung His head for your grief. He endured the darkness so you could enjoy the presence of the Father's light. It is in His presence that your heart will be made whole.

Jesus knew separation from the Father would be the worst sorrow you could ever experience. Therefore, He did not allow the grief of His situation to distract Him. He did not lick His wounds, talk about how bad He felt, or sulk in sadness. Jesus did not look back. Jesus kept His eyes on the Father's will and focused upon the joy set before Him. This joy was saving you.

> *Looking unto Jesus the author and finisher of our faith;* ***who for the joy that was set before him*** *endured the cross, despising the shame, and is set down at the right hand of the throne of God.* (Hebrews 12:2) (Emphasis mine)

Window of Faith

Spending time with your Savior Christ Jesus will do miracles in your season of mourning. Open God's Holy Word and allow His Spirit to release you into fresh horizons. Deeper insight on God's immeasurable grace will replace your grief. People who have small windows receive a certain amount of light, but those with larger frames have rooms greatly illuminated. Consider broadening your view, and allow Jesus to unveil His gift of copious healing.

Noah had a window in the ark, and after forty days of rain he propped it open. He released a raven first, and then a dove, to see if land was in sight. Without giving up, Noah kept looking out the window and releasing the dove. Confined within the ark, Noah knew firsthand the effects of grief. Sin caused the world to be filled with the Father's tears. And yet, Noah's faith for restoration was relentless. What if Noah didn't dare to peek out the window to see God's grace for a new start? Noah would have missed out on experiencing a second chance.

> *So it came to pass, at the end of forty days, that Noah opened the window of the ark which he had made. Then he sent out a raven, which kept going to and fro until the waters had dried up from the earth. He also sent out from himself a dove, to see if the waters had receded from the face of the ground. But the dove found no resting place for the sole of her foot, and she returned into the ark to him, for the waters were on the face of the whole earth. So he put out his hand and took her, and drew her into the ark to himself. And he waited yet another seven days, and again he sent the dove out from the ark. Then the dove came to him in the evening, and behold, a freshly plucked olive leaf was in her mouth; and Noah knew that the waters had receded from the earth. So he waited yet another seven days and sent out the dove, which did not return again to him anymore. (Genesis 8:6-12)*

Please keep returning to the window of God's Word for your revelation. Lose not sight of healing grace and new opportunities. Your steadfast faith in Christ Jesus will enhance as your sorrow is released like a dove.

Bright Clouds Bring Consolation

Sorrowing tears pour out from dark clouds of depression. While mourning, it is difficult to develop the motivation to dive into the day. Each step is like moving through a swampy bog filled with murmurings of melancholy. Looking up into the Heavens, your heart longs for a lifting of this misery. As the storms thunder anger and hurt within, your cries beckon an answer from above. Without warning, a bright cloud permeates into your misery.

Miraculously, the disturbance of sadness subsides. Refreshing, gentle showers begin to pour into your pain. The gloomy clouds dissipate in the presence of Christ. Bereavement is banned as healing arrives. When Jesus is invited into the gales of grief, the waves of unrestful feelings obey.

So the men marveled, saying, What manner of man is this, that even the winds and the sea obey him! Matthew 8:27

Doubt not; the turmoil will disappear. Your bright cloud speaks to the hurricane of hurt. Unseen is your Savior lining the gray with His grace. It pleases the Father to share His Son's healing sacrifice with you.

> *Behold, a bright cloud overshadowed them: and behold a voice out of the cloud, which said, This is my beloved Son, in whom I am well pleased; hear ye him. Matthew 17:5*

Too often people in sorrow want to be in control. Hesitate not to call upon Him in the day when death interrupts your life and leaves you destitute. You can't conquer this raging tempest alone.

> *And call upon me in the day of trouble: I will deliver thee, and thou shalt glorify me. (Psalm 50:15)*

When loss leaves dark clouds upon your life, *ask* the LORD to bring you bright clouds of consolation. Depend on the One who will dismiss your depression like showers of rain watering the drought of your heart.

Zechariah 10:1 states, *Ask ye the LORD rain in the time of the latter rain; so the LORD shall make bright clouds, and give them showers of rain, to every one grass in the field.*

Who Will Remain the Same?

The earth we walk on, the heavens we gaze upon, and the people we rely upon will all fade away. We hate to imagine the things we see will one day slip from our sight. We read obituaries and attend funerals, yet fail to believe it will happen to us. So we continue on as before, grasping for security and fighting against change.

Facing loss shoots cannonballs of rebellion into the sphere of our reality. The battle rages with spewing emotion. We seek cooling ponds to soak our sorrow in, only to see a reflection of truth. Until surrendered to eternal love, insecurity stirs our souls.

No person or place, but only our personal Lord and Savior, Jesus Christ, will settle our fragile hearts. Fall into the arms of the One who won't change. Find His hand and walk into your day knowing He will never leave you nor forsake you.

And the LORD, he it is that doth go before thee; he will be with thee, he will not fail thee, neither forsake thee: fear not, neither be dismayed. (Deuteronomy 31:8)

One day your last breath will beckon you far beyond this world. Rejoice as you pass by grief, which is left at Heaven's Gate.

About the Author

Theresa Ellison has served as a Hospice/Hospital Chaplain, Bereavement Coordinator and Mental Health/Chemical Addictions Counselor. Throughout her career, grief has been the chief complaint disrupting numerous lives. Inspired to offer the heavenly perspective on grief, her prayer is to present Jesus to every grieving heart.

Theresa has settled in Northern Minnesota, where she enjoys the outdoor life with her husband, and their German Shepherd.

website: www.blessmyblog.com

CPSIA information can be obtained
at www.ICGtesting.com
Printed in the USA
LVHW090845051020
667943LV00002B/143